The Yoga of Sri Krishna

BIHAR SCHOOL OF YOGA
50 years
1963–2013
GOLDEN JUBILEE

WORLD YOGA CONVENTION 2013
GANGA DARSHAN, MUNGER, BIHAR, INDIA
23rd–27th October 2013

The Yoga of Sri Krishna

Swami Niranjanananda Saraswati

Discourses from the Yogadrishti (Yogavision) series of satsangs at Paduka Darshan Sannyasa Peeth, Munger, from 17th to 18th February 2012

Yoga Publications Trust, Munger, Bihar, India

Published by Yoga Publications Trust
First edition 2012

ISBN: 978-93-81620-14-4

Publisher and distributor: Yoga Publications Trust, Ganga Darshan, Munger, Bihar, India.

Website: www.biharyoga.net
www.rikhiapeeth.net

Printed at Aegean Offset Printers, Greater Noida

Dedication

To our guru Sri Swami Satyananda Saraswati
who continues to inspire and guide us
on our spiritual journey.

Contents

Yoga of Situation Management

17 February 2012

The stories of Sri Krishna's childhood, young adult life and role in the Mahabharata war are well known. What is less known about him is the long and arduous sadhanas he performed on several occasions in *ekanta vasa*, solitary retreats.

There are several periods in Sri Krishna's life when he was involved in intense sadhanas, through which he attained mastery in yoga. That is why he is known as 'Yogeshwara', lord of yoga. There are only two people who have been given the title of 'Yogeshwara' in history. One is Shiva, the first exponent of yoga and the hero of all aspiring yogis. He is called *Yogishwara*, lord of the yogis. Sri Krishna is known as *Yogeshwara*, which means that he is the lord of yoga as a practice, lifestyle, philosophy and understanding.

For twelve years Sri Krishna lived in the Sandipani ashram and under his guru's tutelage studied the Vedas, Vedangas, practised yoga sadhanas, karma yoga, jnana yoga, bhakti yoga, raja yoga, hatha yoga, among other sadhanas. Finally, he performed pashupata yoga to invoke Shiva, in order to have a son by his third wife, Jambavati.

The instructions in the *Bhagavad Gita* were given towards the end of his life when he had perfected all the sadhanas. Here he imparts a series of yogic teachings to Arjuna which are more relevant for situation management rather than spiritual development. However, while he taught Arjuna simple methods to manage practical problems, embedded within his instructions are also several spiritual sadhanas.

The Mahabharata

The *Bhagavad Gita* was narrated to Arjuna during the Mahabharata war, which took place about 5,500 years ago. Yet, the beauty of the book lies in that it speaks of eternal issues. If you look at your own life today, you will find that you are undergoing the same experiences that Arjuna experienced and discussed with Sri Krishna on the battlefield. The solutions that Sri Krishna offered are also as relevant today as they were thousands of years ago.

The story of the *Mahabharata* revolves around two groups of cousins, five brothers called the Pandavas and one hundred brothers called the Kauravas. The Kauravas develop an intense dislike towards the five Pandavas. Over time, the dislike turns into hatred and the ultimate outcome is a war between the two parties.

As the two sides prepare to engage in war, on one side of the battlefield are arrayed the five brothers, along with their allies, supporters and armies. On the other side are the one hundred Kaurava brothers along with their friends, allies and armies. All stand there, holding their weapons aloft, ready to kill each other.

One of the Pandavas, Arjuna, is a great archer. Sri Krishna is his charioteer during the war. As the great battle is about to commence, Arjuna asks Sri Krishna to drive the chariot between the two armies, so he can see all the people who have come ready to fight and kill each other. Sri Krishna places the chariot in the middle of the two armies and Arjuna sees his own brothers with their allies arrayed before him in army formations. On the other side he sees everyone else: the hundred Kaurava cousins, their allies, supporters, family members, uncles, grandparents, nephews, sons . . . anybody who is able to fight is present. Seeing this, Arjuna suddenly experiences deep pangs of grief, and goes through a state of dejection and depression.

The cause of Arjuna's grief is the sight of his own family and friends prepared to fight and kill each other.

Arjuna's dejection

As a warrior, Arjuna has fought in many wars and never felt grief. The difference on this occasion is that on the battlefield he sees people not as enemies, but as his own relatives: uncles, sons, nephews, parents, grandparents and friends. Arjuna feels a natural attachment for these people who have been a part of the Pandavas' life since their birth. This attachment becomes the cause of his deepening grief. Every memory of the relationships, all the physical, intellectual, emotional and playful memories, every impression or *pratyaya*, surfaces in his mind. Arjuna cannot handle it.

He sits down dejected and says, "Why fight? What for? Maybe we will win and regain the kingdom, but the kingdom will be devoid of everybody we know. It will be an empty kingdom. What happiness, pleasure or enjoyment will there be without anyone whom we can call our own? For whom are we going to win this kingdom? All our friends, all our supporters are going to die. We call ourselves intellectuals, we formulate religions, virtues, vices and laws; yet, for the sake of greed and desire we are ready to destroy each other completely, knowing well that this civil war will lead to death and destruction of all social norms and structures, and values of the individual, family and society. There will be total chaos, death, destruction, anarchy and poverty. We will inherit an empty kingdom. We are the leaders of society, yet we are gathered to commit the biggest crime of all times; knowingly, wilfully, consciously taking away another person's life. There is no greater sin than killing somebody, there is no greater evil act than killing somebody."

> *Aho bata mahatpaapam kartum vyavasitaa vayam;*
> *Yadraajya sukhalobhena hantum svajanamudyataah.*
>
> Alas! We are involved in a great sin in that we are prepared to kill our kinsmen through greed for the pleasures of a kingdom.
>
> (1:45)

Thinking thus, Arjuna sinks deeper into dejection and depression. He loses his clarity of mind and the will to fight, forgets his karma and dharma, duties and obligations, and sits with his head down in the chariot.

Live your dharma

Sri Krishna has to intervene to lift Arjuna out of this state of despondency. He tries to make him see the bright side of life. Sri Krishna explains to Arjuna the method, process and a sadhana to bring him out of his state of despondency. The instructions that Sri Krishna gives Arjuna are yogic instructions and yogic sadhanas. Befitting his title of 'Yogeshwara', he emphasizes adherence to yoga in life and the perfection of yoga.

To enable Arjuna to work through his state of dejection, depression, despondency and grief, Sri Krishna formulates a specific structure of information and practice, and these are the instructions given in the *Bhagavad Gita*. The *Bhagavad*

Gita is not a religious book or a treatise on philosophy. It is a work which dispels doubts about the dharma that one has to live in life. According to the founding thoughts of the *Bhagavad Gita*, the process of managing life and the cultivation of better qualities are the focus, dharma and journey of life. Yoga is the medium through which one is able to complete this journey.

Attachment

As a human being, everyone goes through states of grief, anxiety, dejection and frustration, and also experiences states of elation, joy, contentment and security. Sometimes you are able to accept situations, at other times you find yourself unable to adapt and adjust to a situation or an environment. Life swings from one extreme to the other.

The pendulum swing of moods, perceptions, thoughts and ideas is something that everyone experiences every day, and everything is centred around relationships with others. Each person cultivates a relationship with other people in different degrees of intensity, and each relationship exists in a world of its own. In a household, the family unit consisting of parents and children is the world to them. Relatives, grandparents, aunts, uncles and their families are added to this world at the second level. The third level is of friends in society, supporters and people who think like you. However, the primary group is still the family. The same feeling does not exist for friends as it does for one of your own.

Attachment is the feeling where you identify with someone as your own. It is the power, the agent through which you recognize somebody as 'my relation, my supporter, my friend, my family, my well-wisher'.

You are affected by those you are connected with. You are not affected by the happiness, pain, suffering, elation or achievements of people who are unknown to you. When you identify with people, and are aware of and influenced by their grief and elation, you become affected. You are affected because of that deep connection which is attachment. Everything that

happens, all your headaches and heartaches in the course of life, whether familial, social, professional or personal, revolves around family, friends, society and known people.

The deep entanglement of attachment with such people and the environment leads to a deluded state of mind which is known as *moha*. You begin to feel that you belong to them and they belong to you, that you have a right over them and they have a right over you. That is moha. Trying to instil and enforce that connection and relationship is moha. The inherent desire, which is a part of life, naturally fuels attachments further, as desires are centred in continuation of lineage or procreation. The inherent desire is to find wellness and prosperity, social and financial security, to be recognized and to have friends and supporters.

Think straight

Sri Krishna explains to Arjuna, "You are experiencing grief, depression and this deluded state of mind because you are not thinking straight. If you can think straight, then these mental conditions will not affect you." Arjuna says, "What do you mean, I am not thinking straight?" Sri Krishna replies, "Primarily, you have forgotten what your commitment and duty is as a member of society. In war, a warrior has to fight just as in a hospital a doctor has to heal and in an ashram the sadhu has to work for the upliftment of others. In each place there is a defined role, known as dharma. You have forgotten the role defined for you in this situation. You cannot negate your karmas. Keep in mind what your obligations, duties and karmas are and where they lie at present. Do not renounce karma. Do not say I am not going to do this or I am not going to do that."

Do as the situation demands, just as you dress according to the weather. In winter you put on a sweater, muffler, hat, socks and gloves. As it gets colder, you increase the layers of clothing, and as summer approaches you reduce the layers. You do not wear a hat, coat, sweater, muffler, socks and gloves in summer or walk around bare-bodied in winter. There is a natural inclination to do the right thing in the right manner at the right time.

Restrain the senses

When the intellect plays a role or is clouded, often the right thing is not done at the right time, and this realization dawns only later. When you are entangled in the throes of attachment, intelligence is clouded, and awareness of dharma is lost. At such times, you must remember your responsibilities, commitment and duty and engage the senses in the appropriate action. The senses must be engaged with control, within defined limits and parameters. Right now, the senses are running amok with nothing controlling them, they are guiding your attention and attraction, and you are simply following their line of sight.

The senses have the power to attract you, as you believe that following the senses will lead you towards pleasure. Sensorial pleasure is what everyone is looking for. Mental, physical and emotional pleasure is what everybody craves. Social pleasure is what everyone cherishes. The senses pull your attention towards pleasure, but the experience of pleasure is impermanent. The experience of happiness is impermanent, as subsequent desires do not allow that experience to remain permanent. If you have one, you want two; if you have two, you want three; if you have three, you want four. An increase of desire, expectation and dependency always takes place. Therefore, engage yourself in physical karma, and by engaging the senses thus, restrain them from running wild and not allowing you to fulfil the demands of the situation.

Sri Krishna says, "There is no question of avoiding karma. Engage yourself in karma and at the same time try to stabilize your mind."

> *Karmanyevaadhikaaraste maa phaleshu kadaachana;*
> *Maa karmaphalaheturbhoormaa te sango'stvakarmani.*
>
> Your right is to work only, but never with its fruits; let not the fruits of actions be your motive, nor let your attachment be to inaction.
>
> *Yogasthah kuru karmaani sangam tyaktvaa dhananjaya;*
> *Siddhyasiddhyoh samo bhootvaa samatvam yoga uchyate.*
>
> Perform action, O Arjuna, being steadfast in yoga, abandoning attachment and balanced in success and failure. Evenness of mind is called yoga.
>
> (2:47–48)

There are three factors that disturb mental behaviour: attachment, fear and anger. Attachment represents connection, association and relationship. Fear represents insecurity, whether financial, personal, familial or social. The thoughts come, "Society is not safe; my family is not safe. I don't have the financial resources to buy food tomorrow or after a month. I don't have enough to pay the bills this month." Such thoughts indicate fear and insecurity. Anger is the third disturbance of the mind, and includes aggression and high anxiety. Anything that stimulates and brings in a state of high anxiety in your nature and character is included in the word 'anger'. The instruction that Sri Krishna gives in order to manage the mind is to reduce desire and restrain anger, fear and attraction. Practise these four things and the mind will become stable.

> *Duhkheshvanudvignamanaah sukheshu vigatasprihah;*
> *Veetaraagabhayakrodhah sthitadheermuniruchyate.*
>
> He whose mind is not shaken by adversity, who does not hanker after pleasures, and who is free from attachment, fear and anger, is called a sage of steady wisdom.
>
> (2:56)

Pratyahara

Sri Krishna next instructs Arjuna in the process of pratyahara. He tells Arjuna, "In order to stabilize the mind, pull the limbs of the mind and the senses inwards, just as the turtle pulls the limbs of its body into its shell."

> *Yadaa samharate chaayam koormo'ngaaneeva sarvashah;*
> *Indriyaaneendriyaarthebhyastasya prajnaa pratishthitaa.*
>
> When, like the turtle which withdraws its limbs on all sides, he (the yogi) withdraws his senses from the sense objects, then his wisdom becomes steady.
>
> (2:58)

Herein is given the definition of the state of pratyahara. The turtle has six limbs sticking out of its shell: two arms, two legs, one tail and one head. Humans function with five senses and the mind, six senses in total. The mind represents the head of the turtle and has to be pulled inside. The five senses represent the arms, legs and tail of the turtle, which must also be pulled in. Withdraw the senses from their corresponding sense objects and pull them within yourself. This is the practice of pratyahara as defined by Patanjali and also as taught to us by our guru, Sri Swami Satyananda.

Pratyahara begins by stilling the physical senses through the practice of kaya sthairyam and by regulating the breath. Breath is the mirror of the mind and mental conditions, and moods are reflected in the breath. When the mind is hyperactive, the breath is rapid, shallow and fast. If the mind is at rest, the breath is long, deep and slow. Therefore, in order to access the mind, regulate the breath. If you can regulate the breath and equalize inhalation and exhalation, through the practice of nadi shodhana pranayama, you can access the mind through breath. To still the physical senses, practise kaya sthairyam. To still the mind use a physical agent: regulation of the length of breath, and then focus the mind on awareness of the Higher Self.

Before you can focus on the awareness of the Higher Self, the layers of the mind have to be traversed. To reach the bottom of the ocean one has to swim through many metres of ocean water. In the same way, one has to go through many layers of the mind to eventually realize and see the presence of higher consciousness within. The deepest part of the ocean is six kilometres deep and you have to swim all the way down. In the same manner, you have to walk through six kilometres of your mind before you come to realize the presence of the Supreme Self within you.

Identify with sattwic karma

When you walk through the six kilometres of your mind, you will encounter different experiences which are instigated by insecurities, anxieties and passion, *kama*. By cultivating self-awareness and knowledge, you learn to manage the behaviour and manifestation of insecurity, anxiety and passion. Sri Krishna instructs Arjuna to continue to focus on performance of karma diligently, effectively, creatively and perfectly. If you are able to perform karma creatively, perfectly, diligently and effectively, without any selfish motive, it will liberate you from the clutches of samskaras and the behaviours of the mind.

If you continue performing karma for selfish reasons, without cultivating awareness and understanding, then it will further bind you into gross awareness. Therefore, continue to perform karma, but identify with the sattwic karma rather than with tamasic or rajasic karma. Do not identify with the limiting, conditioned, detrimental and confining effect of the karma, but identify with the sattwic, luminous, creative and perfect aspect of the karma. Try to remain detached from the karmas, without expectation of a result. Try to maintain mental equipoise while remaining engaged in the world and in karma.

Dedicate karmas to the higher force

Whether you succeed or fail in what you do is not in your control. What you can control is how you act. Therefore, try to act in the best manner possible, using the best of situations that become available. Don't be a soggy face. Try to maintain mental equipoise in success and failure. Sri Krishna says, "Maintain this mental equipoise by remaining fixed on my memory. Any of the senses can disturb the mind, just as a sailboat in the middle of the ocean is moved by a gale, a hurricane, as well as a gentle breeze. Even a soft, gentle breeze of the senses can attract the mind, not only a gale or a hurricane. Absolute awareness has to be maintained as one journeys through the layers of the mind, perfecting pratyahara and performing karma."

Indriyaanaam hi charataam yanmano'nuvidheeyate;
Tadasya harati prajnaam vaayurnaavamivaambhasi.

For the mind which follows in the wake of the wandering senses, carries away its discrimination as the wind (carries away) a boat on the waters.

(2:67)

Mayi sarvaani karmaani sannyasyaadhyaatmachetasaa;
Niraasheernirmamo bhootvaa yudhyasva vigatajvarah.

Renouncing all actions in Me, with the mind centred in the Self, free from hope and egoism, and from (mental) fever, do you fight.

(3:30)

Arjuna asks Sri Krishna, "What do I identify with, so I can perform karma in the correct manner?" Sri Krishna answers that karma which is in accordance with dharma and natural human justice should be performed. Karma which follows the mandates of dharma should be performed, as it will always uplift the individual and the surroundings. Learn to identify with those actions, perceptions and attitudes which will help bring creativity in life. Arjuna asks, "How do I improve karmas?" Sri Krishna answers, "There is no question of improving anything. Only dedicate your karmas to me."

The same teaching was given to Sri Swamiji when he asked his guru, Swami Sivananda, "What do I do after I take sannyasa?" Swami Sivananda replied, "You have to carry on doing the same things that you have been doing until today. You have been cleaning the ashram daily. You have been looking after the office, the income, expenditure, kitchen, press and correspondence?" Sri Swamiji said, "Yes." Swami Sivananda said, "Continue doing the same. There is no change in your duty or karma." Then Sri Swamiji said, "In that case, I can go home and continue to do my karma." Swami Sivananda said, "No. The difference is that when you perform karma thinking you are the cause of that action and expect a result, then that karma is binding. In the ashram you perform karmas, but you are not responsible for the result. Your duty is to act in the best manner possible, but the result, whether positive or negative, belongs to the guru. Do your best and do not have any expectations from the karma."

According to the ashram tradition, a sannyasin must live for twelve years in the guru's ashram doing guru seva. It is not sadhana, but guru seva that is mandated, as the guru is able to connect you with the right way of action. When karma is expressed with creativity and perfection, it becomes karma yoga. However, you have to be aware of and manage the responses and reactions that karma generates. If you do well, other people will become jealous and try to pull you down. If you do badly, other people will still complain and want to pull you down. That is the law of life. Nobody says anything good about anybody else, but is ever ready with complaints. The best way is not to react to praise or abuse. If somebody tells you, "You are a dog", rather than getting angry and barking at that person, if you say, "Wonderful, only a dog recognizes another dog," the moment passes in a light manner, without anger. In this manner, reactions have to be managed and instead of becoming the cause of grief, they should become the cause of laughter.

Thy will be done

If you acquire the ability to remain balanced amid praise and abuse, then all your actions are offered to Brahman, the highest Supreme Self, because you become like an instrument that is played. A harmonium can play beautiful music, but not on its own. A musician has to play it. In the same manner, eventually the realization dawns that 'I am not the doer in the world, nor am I the enjoyer'.

As long as the attention is focused on self-oriented and selfish reasons, motives and purposes, you are the doer and the enjoyer. However, once the attitude, identification and perception shifts from a self-centred focus to the realization and understanding that you are not the doer, surrender of the limited ego to the Higher Self begins.

Meditation, a tool to reach the Higher Self

Sri Krishna's entire teaching to Arjuna emphasizes the use of meditation as a tool to withdraw the senses, and to develop awareness and knowledge. Meditation is not cutting off from the world, but becoming more involved with the world. Develop knowledge of the situation, your duty, commitment, obligation, mood and intention. Manage your passion, fear, anger, attraction and attachment. Become active creatively. Develop and expand your awareness so that you increase your knowledge. Meditation is used to increase jnana, awareness of oneself, of how one behaves at different moments and in different situations. Restrain the wild movement of the senses by fixing the mind, consciousness and mental attention, and try to attain the experience of the Higher Self by going through the layers of the mind. Remain true to your goal; perfect pratyahara. Do not let the different expressions and experiences of the mind divert your attention and awareness. Just as a wisp of wind can move the sails of the boat in the ocean, in the same manner, a simple diversion at any level will shake your boat as well.

Pranayama

Arjuna poses a question, "How do I control passion? You have spoken of antar mouna as the process to manage conditions and states of fear, anxiety and attachments, but how do I manage passions?" Sri Krishna gives Arjuna a sadhana: to fix the mind at the eyebrow centre and regulate the breath, making the inhalation and exhalation as long as possible,

and during the gap between inhalation and exhalation, focus the awareness on the inner Self. This is the practice of nadi shodhana pranayama.

By placing the two fingers at the eyebrow centre, a pressure point is created to enable the mind to become fixed at the eyebrow centre. Regulate the breath to a minimum of twenty-four *matras*, units, per incoming and outgoing breath. Each matra is like a second. The Gayatri mantra of twenty-four matras is used to practise nadi shodhana pranayama:

Om tatsavitur varenyam bhargo devasya dheemahi dhiyo yo nah prachodayaat.

Twenty-four matras make one inhalation. This is the training that Sri Krishna imparts to keep the mind fixed.

Sparshaankritvaa bahirbaahyaamshchakshushchaivaantare bhruvoh;
Praanaapaanau samau kritvaa naasaabhyantarachaarinau.

Yatendriya manobuddhirmunirmokshaparaayanah;
Vigatechchhaabhayakrodho yah sadaa mukta eva sah.

Shutting out (all) external contacts and fixing the gaze between the eyebrows, equalizing the outgoing and incoming breaths moving within the nostrils, with the senses, the mind and the intellect always controlled, having liberation as his supreme goal, free from desire, fear and anger – the sage is verily liberated forever.

(5:27–28)

When you regulate the breath, brainwaves are affected. High alpha and theta waves predominate and with these two waves predominating, the nervous system and mental dimension experience a state of relaxation and a balance of energies, physical, sensorial, mental, emotional, psychic and spiritual. When you practise slow pranayama the body feels different. With fast pranayama and rapid breathing the body condition is different. The word which has been used in the *Bhagavad Gita* indicates long, deep breathing and lengthening the ratio of breath. Slow and deep breathing relaxes the physical structure, the nervous system and the brain. This relaxed condition in turn influences mental and psychological behaviour. Many therapists use pranayama to create a change in the mental behaviour of mentally challenged people. In the early days, I have also used pranayama in a prison and in a catatonic care centre. Therefore, I can vouch for the efficacy of the method. By balancing the energies of ida and pingala, positive personality changes come about.

Sri Krishna speaks of pranayama as a method of managing the hyperactive and passionate mental behaviours. Passion is not always sensorial, sensual or sexual. Passion is any desire or thought that dominates the mind. It represents a condition of mental behaviour in which one item becomes predominant and highlighted, and all reactions, responses, actions, thoughts and interactions revolve around that one particular thought or idea. This sustained mental function is known as passion, which can be directed and used for anything. An artist can become a passionate artist, a sculptor can become a passionate sculptor, a yogi can become a passionate yogi. That energy, awareness and mentality can take any form and shape, negative or positive, tamasic or sattwic. By regulating the prana shakti, pranayama balances the extreme behaviour of the passions and levels out the mental extremes.

In this way, Sri Krishna teaches ways of managing different types of situations which everyone encounters on an everyday basis, using very simple practices of yoga and ideas to cultivate understanding and awareness.

Yoga of Higher Realization

18 February 2012

The *Bhagavad Gita* begins with the story of a person in grief, who finds it difficult to decide what his dharma is. His difficulty and indecision have arisen due to attachments and desires. These have given birth to grief, dejection and depression. Before him stands Sri Krishna, who sees this person forgetting his dharma, falling into a depressive and grief-stricken state of mind, and undergoing a nervous breakdown affecting his entire personality.

Sri Krishna has no choice but to try and bring Arjuna out of this physical and psychological condition, so that he can follow his dharma and discover the appropriate understanding which will lead him towards success in life. Sri Krishna continuously inspires Arjuna the warrior, to become active and involved in the performance of his duties. He repeatedly reminds Arjuna to perform his duty with detachment, perfection and creativity, and to express and give his best.

Action without attachment

In the early days, when I came to the ashram, one of the instructions that Sri Swamiji gave me was to give my best. He said, "Niranjan, believe that every day is a new day and that there is always something to learn in that new day. The day that has gone, does not come back again. Always be alert to learn whatever you can every day." Sri Swamiji inspired me to become active mentally, to keep my eyes open and my awareness expanded to see the new lessons I could learn and imbibe every day. That process continues even today. It is one way of understanding involvement in karma.

Sri Krishna keeps goading Arjuna into action again and again, from the second to the ninth chapter of the *Bhagavad Gita*. As he pushes him to perform action, he also instructs him to keep actions and attachments separate.

> *Yogasannyastakarmaanam jnaanasanchhinnasamshayam;*
> *Aatmavantam na karmaani nibadhnanti dhananjaya.*
>
> He who has renounced actions by yoga, whose doubts are rent asunder by knowledge, and who is self-possessed, actions do not bind him, O Arjuna!
>
> *Tasmaadajnaanasambhootam hritstham jnaanaasinaatmanah;*
> *Chhittvainam samshayam yogamaatishthottishtha bhaarata.*
>
> Therefore, with the sword of knowledge (of the Self) cut asunder the doubt of the self born of ignorance, residing in thy heart, and take refuge in yoga; arise, O Arjuna!
>
> (4:41–42)

Sri Krishna advises, keep actions and the desire for action separate. Keep actions and the results of actions separate. Do not let anything affect your creative and natural skill and ability to perform. If at any point there is an expectation from the action, for the result and the gain or loss, the mind will become entangled in that action and will reap the consequences of either grief or elation. The mind will continue to swing between grief and happiness. This swing of the mind will always keep it disturbed, distracted and looking outwards. The more you look outwards, the more entangled the senses become with sense objects. The more the senses are entangled with sense objects the more desires and attachments arise, and the mind is once again buffeted by the winds of loss and gain. The cycle of grief starts anew.

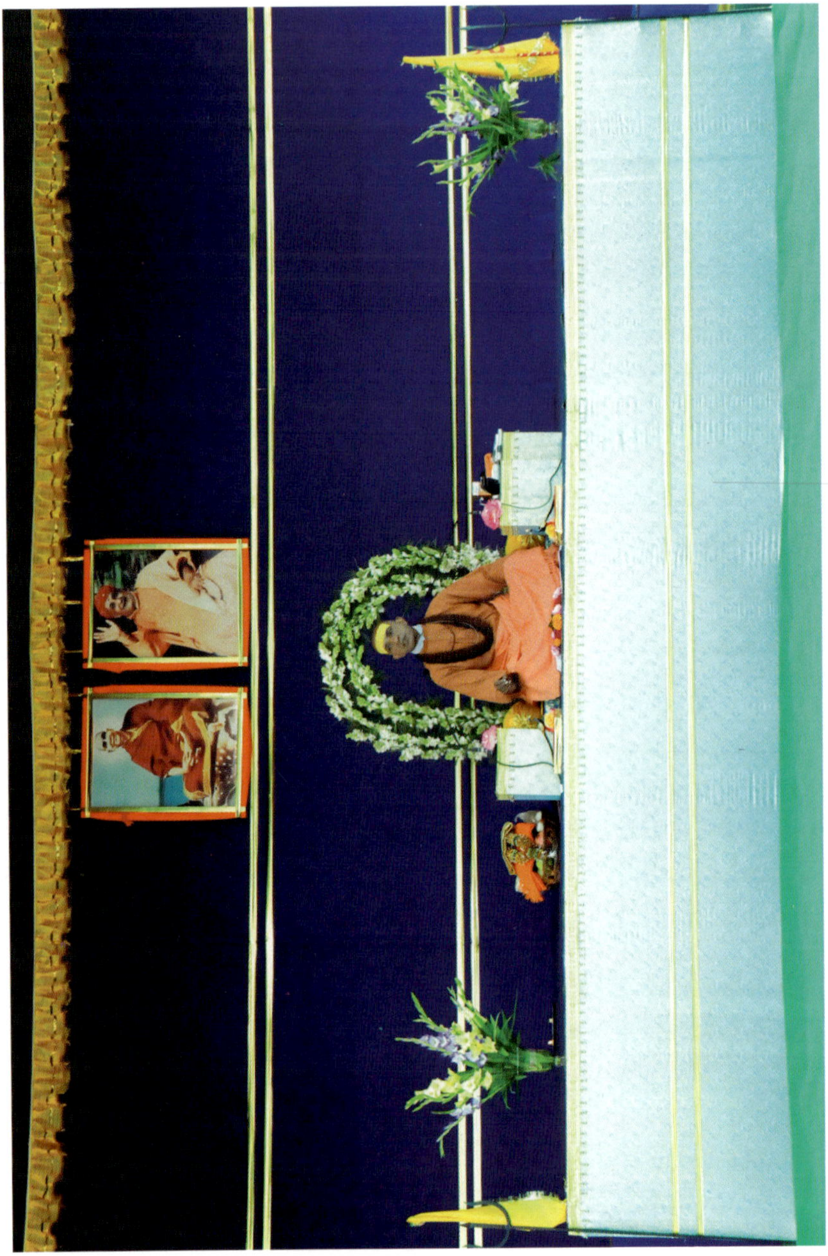

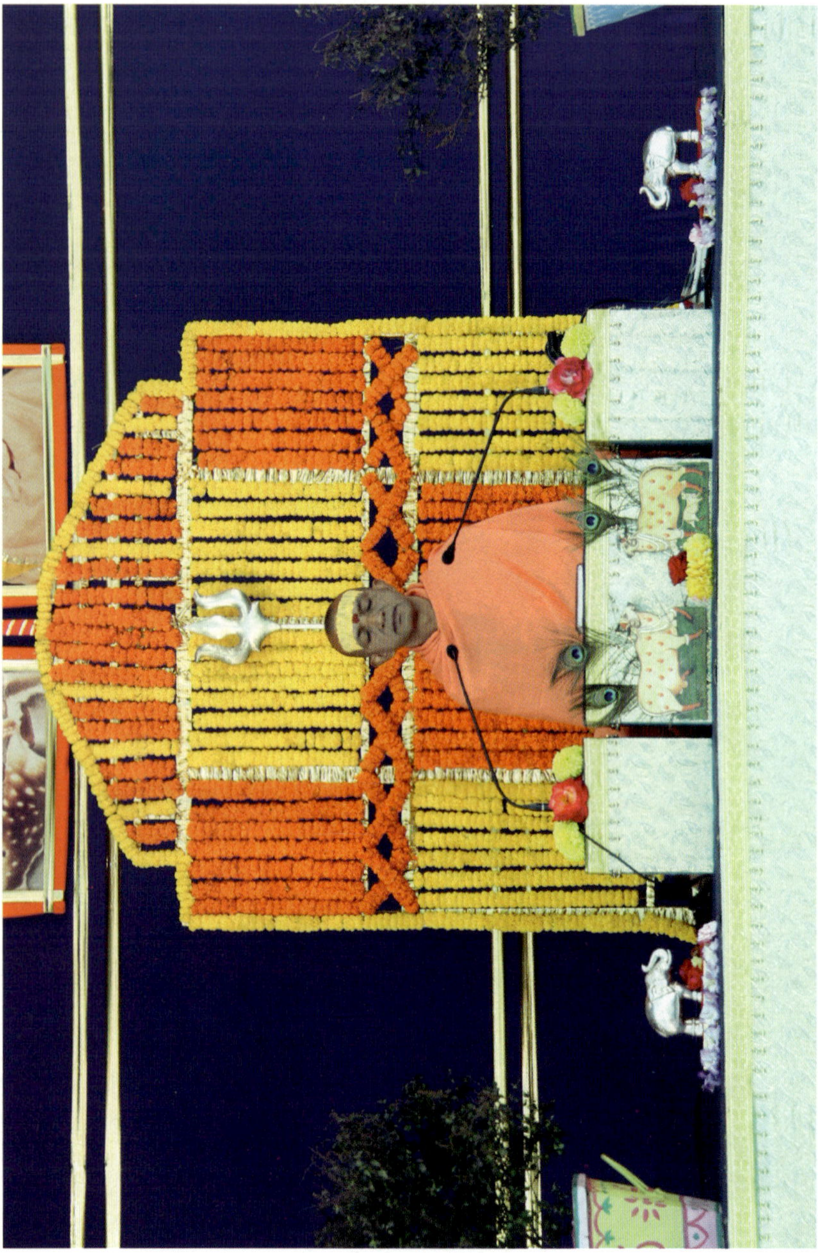

Maintain mental balance

Involve yourself physically, mentally, wholeheartedly in the present moment, in the karma that you are performing, according to time, space, location, environment and the need of the present moment. If you are aware of the present karma and try to do your best, then that karma will free you from the negative and the binding conditionings, expressions, behaviours and moods of the senses.

The senses are both physical and internal; the internal senses are the mental vrittis. One must cultivate detachment towards the behaviour of both. On the one hand, Sri Krishna is constantly inspiring Arjuna to become involved in action. On the other, he is reminding him to not fall into the trap of grief, delusion, dejection and depression, but to find mental balance. In order to find mental balance, Sri Krishna guides Arjuna in the process of pratyahara.

Abhyasa and vairagya

Arjuna asks Sri Krishna, "Do you think by practising pratyahara I can still the nature of my mind? The nature of the mind is always dynamic, active, moving from one object of perception and understanding to another. The mind is very dissipated, distracted and disturbed. It is not possible to stop the constantly moving wind, how can it be possible to stop the mind?" Sri Krishna answers, "Yes, it is possible." This ability comes with abhyasa and vairagya. *Abhyasa* means practice, *vairagya* means detachment. In the *Yoga Sutras*, Maharshi Patanjali describes what abhyasa is: constant, continuous practice and effort sustained over a long period, and done with faith. Through abhyasa one can attain mastery or perfection of the practice.

> *Abhyaasavairaagyaabgyaam tannirodhah*
>
> The stopping of that (five vrittis) by abhyasa and vairagya.
>
> *Tatra sthitau yatno'bhyaasah*
>
> Of the two to be established in the endeavour is abhyasa.
>
> *Sa tu deerghakaala nairantaryasatkaaraasevito dridhabhoomih*
>
> It becomes firmly grounded by being continued for a long time with reverence, without interruption.
>
> (*Yoga Sutras*, 1:12–14)

Sri Krishna has said the same thing: it is possible to manage the upheavals of the mind with practice. Practice means following a system, a sequence of changing the perception and awareness, and observing the physical, psychological and spiritual dimensions of human experience. Vairagya is detachment from actions.

> *Asamshayam mahaabaaho mano durnigraham chalam;*
> *Abhyaasena tu kaunteya vairaagyena cha grihyate.*
>
> Undoubtedly, O mighty-armed Arjuna, the mind is difficult to control and restless; but, by practice and by detachment it may be restrained.
>
> (6:35)

With abhyasa and vairagya it becomes possible to still the agitations of the mind. Just as in a closed room where there is not a whisper of wind, a candle flame burns steadily without shaking or moving, in the same manner, with restraint of the senses, abhyasa and vairagya, and knowing that the effects of attachment are attraction, insecurity and anxiety, you can gradually reduce the movement of the mind.

Passion: obsession of the mind

Sri Krishna also identifies a specific behaviour of the mind: the obsessive passionate behaviour. Passion denotes a state or condition of mind where you hang on to one thing, one idea, one thought or object and begin to revolve around that. If the mind begins to think of sensorial pleasure, the need for sensorial pleasure is highlighted. If the mind thinks of emotional pleasure, the need for emotional pleasure is highlighted. In this passionate state of mind, one obsession can taint and colour the entire area of the mind and change the total human behaviour. This state is known as *kama,* passion.

> *Aavritam jnaanametena jnaanino nityavairinaa;*
> *Kaamaroopena kaunteya dushpoorenaanalena cha.*
>
> O Arjuna, wisdom is enveloped by this constant enemy of the wise in the form of passion, which is unappeasable as fire.

Indriyaani mano buddhirasyaadhishthaanamuchyate;
Etairvimohayatyesha jnaanamaavritya dehinam.

The senses, mind and intellect are said to be its seat; through these it deludes the embodied by veiling his wisdom.

(3:39–40)

Passion is not only sensorial, sensual or sexual; it is also emotional, intellectual, and spiritual. It is an intensity of desire, intention or thought seen in the intensity of expression and action. Passion resides in the senses, the mind and intelligence, and disturbs the pranas of the body. You cannot control passion, but you can manage the pranas, and through the pranas control passion. Therefore, Sri Krishna instructs Arjuna in the practice of pranayama.

Pranayama: method to overcome passions

To reduce attachment, to reduce mental and sensorial attractions, to overcome insecurities and fears, to manage anxieties and aggression of character, Sri Krishna teaches the method of pratyahara. To overcome passion which disturbs the energies and forces of body and mind he teaches pranayama. The basic pranayama is nadi shodhana, the simplest and also the most intense. As you increase the length of your respiration, with continued slow and deep breathing, the flows in ida and pingala are balanced.

For many months in Rikhia, while Sri Swamiji performed his austerities, he practised pranayama for eight hours a day, for many months. During this time his entire personality changed. With the lengthening and regulation of the incoming and outgoing breath, the energies of ida and pingala, *prana shakti*, vital energy, and *chitta shakti*, mental energy, become balanced. That is the moment when one can become free of all the influences of karmas. The example confirms what Sri Krishna points at in his instructions on the practice of pranayama.

Naam smaran

Sri Krishna imparts a series of instructions for another, higher type of meditation: remembrance of the name of God. He explains that this practice should be performed in a clean space, where there is a feeling of purity. Place an asana there, either made of grass, animal skin or cloth. Sit down on the asana, hold the body firm and perfectly still, and gaze at the nose tip. This is called *nasikagra drishti*. While you gaze at the nose tip, take your awareness away from everything else. With your mind fixed on your inner self, remember God.

How does one remember God? Either by remembering a name or a form. These are the two methods for recognition of anything. If you think of somebody, the person's form appears in front of your eyes. If you think or speak of somebody, the name comes to the tip of the tongue. Any manifest object is always identified by either name or form. For God, the name is the mantra. By remembering and repeating the mantra or by focusing the mind at chidakasha on the image of the ishta devata, one cultivates awareness of the higher Self. These are the two common practices of meditation, mantra meditation and symbol meditation.

The two methods can be practised separately; however, they are most effective when practised together. While chanting the mantra, focus on the symbol or image. In this way, the mind is fixed in two dimensions. At the visual level it is seeing the image and at the thought level it is repeating the mantra. At the sensorial level the mind is seeing the image and at the mental level it is repeating the mantra. In this manner, Sri Krishna instructs Arjuna into mantra sadhana.

Shuchau deshe pratishthaapya sthiramaasanamaatmanah;
Naatyuchchhritam naatineecham chailaajinakushottaram.

Tatraikaagram manah kritvaa yatachittendriyakriyah;
Upavishyaasane yunjyaadyogamaatmavishuddhaye.

Samam kaayashirogreevam dhaarayannachalam sthirah;
Samprekshya naasikaagram svam dishashchaanavalokayan.

Prashaantaatmaa vigatabheerbrahmachaarivrate sthitah;
Manah samyamya machchitto yukta aaseeta matparah.

In a clean spot, having established a firm seat of his own, neither too high nor too low, made of a cloth, a skin or kusha grass. There, having made the mind one-pointed, with the actions of the mind and the senses controlled, let him, seated on the seat, practise yoga for the purification of the self. Let him firmly hold his body, head and neck erect and perfectly still, gazing at the tip of his nose, without looking around. Serene-minded, fearless, firm in the vow of a brahmachari, having controlled the mind, thinking of Me and balanced in mind, let him sit, having Me as his supreme goal.

(6:11–14)

Manifest divinity

Arjuna asks, "With everything that you have told me, many of my doubts have been cleared, but you keep saying, focus on you. What does this mean? Focus on you as God or as an individual? As God you are impersonal and as an individual you are my friend. Who are you?" Sri Krishna then describes his divine nature. The instructions and guidelines on yoga stop and the description of the divine nature, a devotee and a jnani begins, as well as a description of the dimension we live in.

When Arjuna asks, "Who are you? What are your attributes?" Sri Krishna answers him in the tenth chapter, describing his divine attributes and says, "I am endowed with these attributes and so are you. The only difference is that I am aware of them and they are awake within me, while you are not aware of them, they are dormant within you. I pervade the entire universe and, at the same time, I am confined to this body as your friend."

Arjuna says, "I believe that you are contained in the entire universe. Can you show me your universal form?" Through shaktipat, Sri Krishna enables Arjuna to see his universal form. Arjuna is speechless; he sees all the galaxies, the multiverses, all the stars, suns, moons, planets, everything contained in Sri Krishna's body. He sees different types of life forms: elemental forms, physical forms of people, animals and insects. He sees the entire creation in Sri Krishna's body, all the people who have been born in the past, all those living in the present and all who will be born in the future. With this hallucinogenic experience, Arjuna goes into a stupor and says to Sri Krishna, "I am frightened. I am afraid of your universal form. Come back to your human form, the form that I identify with all the time as my friend."

Qualities of a bhakta

When Sri Krishna returns to his human form, Arjuna says, "You have shown me that ultimately, we all emanate from and merge in you. I have also seen that there are different types of people in the world who adore, worship and try to attain you. In this group there are two types. One, who believe that you are *nirakara*, without form, and worship the formless God. Two, those who worship you as having a form, in different forms. Which is better? Adoring, worshipping, and identifying with the formless, or with the form? Which *bhakta*, devotee, is better?"

Sri Krishna replies, "Neither is better nor worse than the other. They are different paths. According to personal inclination, people adopt one path or the other. However, expressing devotion and faith is not bhakti, adoring and worshipping me all the time is not bhakti. A true bhakta or devotee is a person who has attained a higher state of mind and perception. The person who has attained this higher state of mind is dear to me because he is endowed with special qualities which do not allow him to see any distinction between me and my creation. He sees me in everything and everything in me. He is friendly and compassionate to everybody, as he sees me in everything. He is without ego and arrogance, as he sees me in everybody."

> *Adveshtaa sarvabhootaanaam maitrah karuna eva cha;*
> *Nirmamo nirahankaarah samaduhkhasukhah kshamee.*
>
> *Santushtah satatam yogee yataatmaa dridhanishchayah;*
> *Mayyarpitamanobuddhiryo madbhaktah sa me priyah.*
>
> He who hates no creature, who is friendly and compassionate to all, who is free from attachment and egoism, balanced in pleasure and pain, and forgiving, ever content, steady in meditation, possessed of firm conviction, self-controlled, with mind and intellect dedicated to Me, he, My devotee, is dear to Me.
>
> (12:13–14)

In this manner, Sri Krishna defines the characteristics of a devotee who has gone beyond external and physical worship, and who has begun to realize the existence of the divine being and power in every speck and atom of creation.

> *Yasmaannodvijate loko lokaannodvijate cha yah;*
> *Harshaamarshabhayodvegairmukto yah sa cha me priyah.*
>
> He by whom the world is not agitated and who cannot be agitated by the world, and who is freed from joy, envy, fear and anxiety – he is dear to Me.

Anapekshah shuchirdaksha udaaseeno gatavyathah;
Sarvaarambhaparityaagee yo madbhaktah sa me priyah.

He who is free from wants, pure, expert, unconcerned, and untroubled, renouncing all undertakings or commencements – he who is (thus) devoted to Me, is dear to Me.

Yona hrishyati na dveshti na shochati na kaangkshati;
Shubhaashubhaparityaagee bhaktimaan yah sa me priyah.

He who neither rejoices, nor hates, nor grieves, nor desires, renouncing good and evil, and who is full of devotion, is dear to Me.

Samah shatrau cha mitre cha tathaa maanaapamaanayoh;
Sheetoshnasukhaduhkheshu samah sangavivarjitah.

He who is the same to foe and friend, and in honour and dishonour, who is the same in cold and heat and in pleasure and pain, who is free from attachment,

Tulyanindaastutirmaunee santushto yena kenachit:
Aniketah sthiramatir bhaktimaan me priyo narah.

He to whom censure and praise are equal, who is silent, content with anything, homeless, of a steady mind, and full of devotion – that person is dear to Me.

(12:15–19)

Atmabhava

Sri Swamiji says the same thing. Cultivate *atmabhava*, see yourself in others. If you look deep within yourself, beyond skin and bones, blood and muscles, you will see that God is seated within you, he is a tenant in your heart. God lives within you.

Sri Swamiji says if you see a person who is hungry, know that God within that person is also hungry; if you see a person who is sick, know that God within that person is also sick; if you see a person who is happy, know that God within that person is also happy. Through the cultivation of atmabhava, you become capable of seeing that divine spark in yourself and also in others. When you see that divine spark in others, then you are connected with everybody, without separation or duality. There is oneness, a feeling that we all belong to each other, have to support each other and be a source of strength and inspiration to each other.

Yogamaya

When Arjuna hears the description of the characteristics of a devotee, he asks Sri Krishna, "Can you define in which dimension human beings or life forms interact? In how many levels, in how many dimensions?" Sri Krishna replies, "People talk of *prakriti*, nature, but know that prakriti is of two types. One is *jada*, non-sentient, and the other is *chaitanya*, sentient. We are born in the dimension of the insentient nature which is eightfold. Prakriti which is not aware that it exists, jada prakriti, has eight components: the five elements of earth, water, fire, air and ether, and *manas*, rational mind; *buddhi*, intelligence; and *ahamkara*, ego. These are the eight cosmic manifestations which have given birth to every kind of life form in the visible, cognizable creation.

"Sentient prakriti remains with God. It is the prakriti, nature, shakti, or power of yoga. Therefore, this *adishakti*, primary shakti, is known as yogamaya. Yoga brings one closer to the higher nature and maya separates one from the higher nature. Yogamaya has both abilities, to bring one to the dimension of bliss, or to take and engage one in the dimension of grief. As maya, in the realm of the eight aspects of prakriti, this shakti binds one to the dimension of grief and suffering. As yoga, this power lifts one upwards from the dimension of the insentient prakriti to unite with and realize the Higher Self. The dimension where all life forms experience life and undergo the process of evolution takes place in the dimension of the eightfold prakriti."

Bhoomiraapo'nalo vaayuh kham mano buddhireva cha;
Ahankaara iteeyam me bhinnaa prakritirashtadhaa.

Apareyamitastvanyaam prakritim viddhi me paraam;
Jeevabhootaam mahaabaaho yayedam dhaaryate jagat.

Earth, water, fire, air, ether, mind, intellect and egoism – thus is My Nature divided eightfold. This is the inferior prakriti, O mighty-armed (Arjuna)! Know you as different from it My higher prakriti, the very life-element by which this world is upheld.

(7:4–5)

Dhyana

Arjuna asks, "Is it possible to live in this world and ultimately merge with you?" Sri Krishna says, "Yes, there is a method. It is perfecting the state of dhyana, which eventually leads to samadhi. In the state of samadhi the aspirant attains me." Sri Krishna's description of dhyana is also unique. He says, "Sit in a stable and firm posture, fix your awareness at the heart centre, see nothing else, and with each inhalation and exhalation, merge your consciousness with *Om*. Chant the

mantra *Om* with every inhalation and exhalation. This means the chanting is mental, as you cannot chant while inhaling.

Sri Krishna says, "Block and close all the doors of the senses. Do not allow the senses to move at all. Hold your mind firm; do not allow it to move. Concentrate in your heart and merge your mind with breath and the mantra *Om*. If the pranas leave in this state of meditation, there is only merger into me."

> *Sarvadvaaraani samyamya mano hridi nirudhya cha;*
> *Moordhnyaadhaayaatmanah praanamaasthito yogadhaaranaam.*
>
> *Omityekaaksharam brahma vyaaharanmaamanusmaran;*
> *Yah prayaati tyajandeham sa yaati paramaam gatim.*
>
> Having closed all the gates, confined the mind in the heart and fixed the life-breath in the head, engaged in the practice of concentration, uttering the monosyllable *Om* – the Brahman – remembering Me always, he who departs thus, leaving the body, attains to the supreme goal.
>
> (8:12–13)

In this way, Sri Krishna gives indications of both dhyana and samadhi. According to the yoga shastras also, the simplest form of samadhi is attainable with the perfection of awareness of luminosity at the heart centre. Sri Swamiji has mentioned many times that the state of meditation begins with threefold awareness: me the practitioner, the process of meditation, and the goal or aim of meditation. Meditation begins with awareness of three things: I am sitting down, I am practising antar mouna or ajapa japa or dharana, and my aim is to find this. However, in the final stage of meditation, the practitioner and the process both merge with the aim. When the merger occurs, the process disappears, I become the aim, and that is samadhi.

Hari Om Tat Sat

Arjuna asks, "What is the meaning of Om?" Sri Krishna replies, "Om is one of the identities of the higher consciousness. Tat is another identity of that higher consciousness and Sat is another identity of that higher consciousness – Om Tat Sat. *Tat* means that which pervades the entire creation and is contained in everything. *Sat* means the truth which continues to exist and can never be shadowed, blocked or hidden. Truth is permanent and untruth is impermanent. Truth is always what has existed, what exists and will continue to exist in the future. Falsity is something that changes from moment to moment. *Om* is the benevolent power of life.

> *Om tatsaditi nirdesho brahmanastrividhah smritah;*
> *Braahmanaastena vedaashcha yajnaashcha vihitaah puraa.*
>
> Om Tat Sat: this has been declared to be the triple designation of Brahman. By that were created formerly the Brahmanas, the Vedas and the sacrifices.
>
> (17:23)

When Sri Swamiji came to Munger in 1963, the mantra of the yoga movement became *Hari Om Tat Sat*, indicating a link and connection with the Higher Self. The same tradition continues today and will continue tomorrow: identifying the greeting Hari Om Tat Sat with the identity of yoga. It is a greeting which contains the vision and blessings of a saint for Ganga Darshan Yogapeeth.

End of delusion and victory

Finally, Arjuna says, "My delusions have ended. I understand what my dharma is; I am ready to do your bidding." Arjuna is ready to act. The debilitated nerves have become strong, free from nervous depression, weakness and anxiety. He is alert and ready to do Sri Krishna's bidding.

> *Nashto mohah smritirlabdhaa tvatprasaadaanmayaachyuta;*
> *Sthito'smi gatasandehah karishye vachanam tava.*
>
> Destroyed is my delusion as I have gained my memory (knowledge) through your grace, O Krishna! I am firm; my doubts are gone. I will act according to your word.
>
> (18:73)

The *Bhagavad Gita* begins with a question that the blind patriarch, Dhritarashtra, asks his information minister and charioteer, Sanjaya. He says, "Tell me, Sanjaya, what is happening on the field of Kurukhshetra, between my sons and the sons of my brother Pandu, who are gathered there for war?" Sanjaya gives the answer to this question in the last verse of the *Bhagavad Gita*, the 700th verse. He says, "O king, what do you expect? You are asking me what is happening on the battlefield between your son and the sons of Pandu. Don't you know that where there is Yogeshwara, Sri Krishna, and where there is the wielder of the bow, Arjuna, there is only victory, glory, prosperity and wellness?" This is how the *Bhagavad Gita* concludes.

> *Yatra yogeshvarah krishno yatra paartho dhanurdharah;*
> *Tatra shreervijayo bhootirdhruvaa neetirmatirmama.*
>
> Wherever there is Krishna, the lord of yoga, wherever there is Arjuna, the archer, there is prosperity, happiness, victory and appropriateness; such is my conviction.
>
> (18:78)

Hari Om Tat Sat